Relaxing with…

Stars

By Pam Klecan

Panic and Anxiety Series

Book 1

Beginner to Expert

Title ID: 6249706

ISBN-13: 978-1533063274

This book belongs to

_____

I hope you enjoy it!

ACKNOWLDGEMENT

I would like to thank Jan H. for her encouragement, help and expertise.

I would not have even tried to create this book without her, never mind finishing it!

DEDICATION

A big Thank You to my parents who have been supportive

during my long struggle with this disease. You guys are the greatest!

Hi. My name is Pam and I have problems with anxiety and panic disorders.

Does it sound like I am at one of those meetings that are supposed to help people help each other? Well, actually, that is what I am trying to do. Let me give you a little history of how this project started. I received an adult coloring book from my parents for Christmas. The designs were beautiful and I have always been a "crafty" person, so it looked like fun. The book states that it is supposed to help you relax and calm down. Well, I was having a not-so-calm day and thought I would try using the book to relax. Now, I don't know about you but when I am feeling anxious, my hands shake. And shaky hands don't work well coloring into the tiny little spots on the mandalas. I started going out the lines and mixing the areas together. What that did was cause my anxiety to get worse and make me feel even more incompetent that I could not even color! This was not working as advertised!

I went looking for something that was for a "beginning colorist" and didn't find anything that I really liked. So, I decided to create an adult coloring book for those with anxiety and panic problems, or you just need to learn how to relax, from someone who knows exactly how it feels.

This book is for you and you can color in it any way you like. Use any instruments that you feel comfortable with, such as crayons, markers, pens, or whatever you want. No one is going to judge you or your pictures. This is for you and only you. Of course, if you want to share, you are welcome to do so. In fact, if you have one you are proud of, there is a place on my website you can upload it to. Scan it into your computer and go to http://relaxingwith.com and click on Upload. Make sure and add your name, so we know who to applaud!

On the other side of this page are your first stars. It is nice and simple to let you experiment with different tools and get the "feel" for coloring. You can color the stars all one color, go for two different colors or just mix it up and do dozens of colors. You can color outside the lines, if you want to. Hey, if you want to add more designs to this page – go for it! It is yours! Your creation!

I will be leaving spaces for you to put in notes about your designs. You might want to state what tools you used or which ones you didn't like. Maybe leave the date of when you did the work. Just make sure you do one thing, especially – Enjoy!

Notes:

_____

_____

How did your first creation go? Are you happy with it? You know what? If you aren't happy with it, that is fine. Now you know what to change the next time. In fact, most artists are never really completely satisfied with their work. They have just learned when to stop!

The next page gives you more stars to work with. Again, this is your picture. You decide if you want to make them all the same color or all different colors. I know that it is hard to make decisions when you feeling anxious or upset, so consider this practice on making a decision and "living" with it.

If you color the stars all one color, then decide that wasn't really what you wanted, you can add more colors by outlining the stars with new colors or adding other decorative items to the page. I can guarantee that it won't mean the end of the world.

This is for no one but you. You are the important one here and you can do whatever you want with the page on the other side. In fact, if you don't like that design, tear it out of the book and throw it away! But first read the other side of the page! ☺

Notes:

_____

_____

_____

_____

_____

_____

_____

Become a worry-slapper. Treat frets like mosquitoes. Do you procrastinate when a bloodsucking bug lights on your skin? "I'll take care of it in a moment." Of course you don't! You give the critter the slap it deserves. Be equally decisive with anxiety.

-Max Lucado

Are you having fun? I hope you are enjoying yourself since that is what this is all about. It is hard to feel anxiety when you are smiling and liking what you are doing.

This next design is three stars that are intertwined. You will need to watch for where they touch and where one is in front of the other. And you can do it! Again, this is your picture and you can color it any way you want. Make them all the same color. Make the stars different colors and show where one is in front of the other. Make them different colors and where they intersect can be another color yet. Whatever you feel comfortable with, because this is to relax you.

Don't forget to leave notes for yourself. You can even use it as a journal area and write how you feel as you do each design.

Notes:

_____

_____

_____

_____

_____

_____

_____

_____

_____

> If you do what you love, it is the best way to relax.
>
> -Christian Louboutin

That last one was a little more complex, wasn't it? You probably needed to concentrate a little more to make sure you got each part of each star the right color or shade. I find that when I have to concentrate, it helps me forget what has been causing the anxiety that day. I hope it worked for you, also.

Well, now that you getting to be more than a beginning colorist, I thought I would give you a design that is a bit harder. Not much but you will have to concentrate. And that is good! You can forget what else is bothering you for a while. Think of coloring as a break from life.

Have fun!

Notes:

_____

_____

_____

_____

_____

_____

_____

_____

_____

Concentrate on your job and you will forget your other troubles.

- William Feather

Things are getting more interesting now, aren't they? Did you use many different colors for that last star or stick with just a few? Whichever way you did was exactly the right way. Remember, these are your creations. You can make them look however you want!

Let's try some new shapes. You got that shape of star down pat, so let's up the game a little and make things more interesting. The new star has more points and is divided differently.

Have fun with this!

Notes:

_____

_____

_____

_____

_____

_____

_____

_____

_____

_____

_____

_____

It's kind of fun to do the impossible.

-Walt Disney

How did you like that last one? I left the middle open so you could add your own design. Are you happy with your creation? If not, then choose different colors or tools for your next one. You are a colorist now, and as every colorist can tell you, it takes practice and patience.

One benefit of coloring for a person that is suffering from anxiety is the chance to calm down by concentrating on your creation. If you are starting to breathe too hard or fast, starting to shake, getting heart palpations, or whatever way your anxiety manifests itself, try to concentrate on your latest creation. Follow the lines with your eyes, consider how it would look with a different color palette or if it needs more colors or less. I find that following the lines of the design helps me calm down. It gives me enough to concentrate on without overwhelming me.

This next design gives you plenty of lines to concentrate on! Also to make your coloring more challenging. Enjoy!

Notes:

_____

_____

_____

_____

_____

_____

_____

_____

Sometimes you can find peace of mind by transferring yourself to different situations. They're just reminders to stay …calm.

-Yves Behar

This next design is to give you a break. It has no intersections but each star does have different divisions. Some are bigger and some are smaller. This is where you have to decide if each star will have the same color scheme or are they all going to be different?

Don't let the decision making process stress you out. I know that when I have decisions I have to make, I can end up like a statue and not be able to think of anything. I find that if I break up the decision to smaller pieces that makes it easier. As an example, don't look at the entire page of stars and try to decide what the whole thing will be. Just pick one star and work on it. That makes the decision smaller and easier to handle. Why don't you give it a try?

Notes:

_____

_____

_____

_____

_____

_____

_____

_____

_____

_____

Do not be afraid to make decisions; do not be afraid to make mistakes.

-Carly Fiorina

We have another new shape of star this time. There are multiple stars that are all the same shape but slightly smaller for each copy, which make is very interesting to follow what goes where!

Again, you can decide if you want to try to follow each star and make it all the same color or to just color each area whatever color looks good. Your design, your decision.

When you look at this next design, does it make you feel anxious? Do you feel paralyzed and like you can't even start it, never mind finish it? This is just like anything else in your life that causes anxiety or panic. Stop, take a breath, and look at it calmly. Pick one small area and complete that. You have now overcome that part of the design, so go after another part! You can do it, especially if you take it a little bit at a time!

Notes:

_____

_____

_____

_____

_____

_____

_____

_____

_____

Concentration is a fine antidote for anxiety.

-Jack Nicklaus

The next stars look a little crazy. In fact, as I was putting this page together, I thought they looked like bacteria under a microscope! Interesting things can come from our imaginations!

Have I mentioned that when you are coloring and things don't work out exactly as you expect, just take a breath and look at your design? See how you can change it to cover the accident. My granddaughter explained to me that when she goes out of the lines, she just makes rainbows all around her design and then it is even prettier! Like Bob Ross, the famous painter and television star, said, "We don't make mistakes, we make happy accidents." So, when your pencil breaks and scoots color outside the line – make a rainbow!

Notes:

_____

_____

_____

_____

_____

_____

_____

_____

_____

_____

And when it rains on your parade, look up rather than down. Without the rain, there would be no rainbow.

-Gilbert K. Chesterton

This next set of stars is letting you work with perspective. Using perspective techniques lets you create something that looks three-dimensional or far away on a two-dimensional piece of paper.

Don't worry, it isn't that hard. It just sounds scary, like a lot of things in life. Once you break it down to its component pieces, it isn't as anxiety-producing as it once was.

Take a look at the next piece. See how it seems to bend? And how the parts in the back look farther away? That is using perspective to give that illusion of distance and shape. A lot of things in life are like that. They are an illusion that causes us anxiety and then it turns out they are just a piece of paper.

Notes:

Limits, like fear, are often illusion.

-Michael Jordan

The last star for this book is your medal to show you have made it all the way through! Congratulations! You have done a wonderful job and I hope you enjoyed yourself as you were working on the different designs.

Look for more Relax With… books at your favorite retailer.

Notes:

_____

_____

_____

_____

_____

_____

_____

_____

_____

> I think the mental victory is worth it as much as a gold medal.
>
> -Cameron van der Burgh

Congratulations! COLORIST Extraordinaire